My Mind's Eye

Vickie Holt

BookLeaf Publishing

India | USA | UK

Presentation by *BookLeaf Publishing*

Web: www.bookleafpub.com

E-mail: info@bookleafpub.com

ISBN: 9789357214216

First edition 2022

*This is dedicated to my sister Valerie. A
true warrior.*

A Fight

Here stands a lonely flag.
Claiming a lonely piece of terra.
Here sits a lonely woman.
Who was once at peace with her lot.
The mists that gathered around her land had
once kept her safe;
but now she felt that they only keep her alone.

The need to be safe that had once dominated her
emotions,
has now been overrun by a need to be whole.
The woman, who did not want to be alone any
longer willed herself to rise.
Her thoughts accelerated her body to move,
and she took one shaky step forward.
Feeling no other resistance she bravely
confronted the mist.

The woman reached out her hand and penetrated
the hazy barrier.
There was nothing there.
Her courage diminishing, her brave thoughts
scrambling.
The possibility that there was nothing beyond
her tiny flag brought the woman to her knees.

The weight of nothing crushing her body down
until her ragged breaths were full of dirt.
This couldn't be happening.

Nothing, couldn't be happening.
She needed something.
Anything.
Other then the lonely flag on the lonely piece of
terra.
Anger was filling her chest.
Disappointment strengthened her body and she
rose once more.

The woman screamed.
Closing her eyes to magnify her feelings,
she blindly propelled herself forward.
The woman was unable to accept, nothing.
She was going to run as far as her legs would
take her.
It was her all against nothing.

She was running.
There had to be something to run to.
She needed something to crash into her.
She needed to feel the weight of it on her body.
Tears began to gather at the corner of her eyes.
Like diamonds they sparkled as they were
wicked away.

So far the woman has reached nothing.
She felt determined to continue on in her quest.
So she would run, forever if she had to.

Bone Tired

It's like there is a familiar dark shadow
that has made it's berth in the shallow parts
of the hollowness in your bones.

And it's screaming.
It wants to be left alone to recover from its deep
wound
that has been afflicted by the monsters in the
world.

When you feel it screaming
the sound travels through the shadow
reverberates past the hollow
and when you open your mouth to relay this
anguish
the only thing you can hear is your own breath
escaping your lips.

The shadow, the hollow, the screaming.
It's coming from your mind.

Cleave

5

What is this constant feeling of inadequacy?
These tall, shadowy creatures that keep
growing ever so steadily and hovering over me.

I am feeling boxed in with nowhere to run.
Now there is just one big black wall on all four
sides.
And my only companion is a bright spotlight
shining down on me.
Looking down with disgusting judgement.

Revealing what's behind my curtain without my
consent.
One bright spot turns into two.
Just like eyes.
Staring down at me.
Boring down into me.

If I'm not careful.
It will sunder me into pieces.

Attack

It's following me again.
I can feel it; can see it lurking in the shadows.
Even if it's only through the corner of my eye.
I can mark the path it takes as it prowls around
me.
My very skin seems to reach out in warning as it
circles me.

There is a heavy drum in my chest.
It beats an odd rhythm that grows faster with
every second.
An ice storm is brewing in my veins.
My body is so cold my breath billows out of my
mouth and chaps my face.

A dark figure steps out of the shadows;
a hooded cloak drapes around t and hangs to the
floor.
I shudder as my mind remembers this cat and
mouse game.
It has chased me before.
The black cloak held out in waiting to
encompass me.

I turn my head and before my body can follow,
I'm caught.

Trapped

I haven't moved in three days.
This cloak of depression has been draped over
me blocking out the world.
I've been laying here in my own filth hoping to
soon get up and live again.

I can hear them, my family.
Everything in me begs to just get up and do
something.
To just participate in what is going on.

This cloak just wraps me tighter with every
wish,
every hope, every beg that flutters into my mind.
It's greedy and doesn't want to let me go.

It's plain as day.
I am one of its possessions.
And it has me trapped.

Purgatory

I'm planning a breakout.
This couch, this blanket has me held hostage for
too long.
I can hear my family talking and laughing and
living around me.
I want to be with them.

I don't want to be in this purgatory with my own
thoughts.
It's getting lonely trying to keep myself
company.
The thoughts keep coming at me from my own
brain and they aren't nice.
They isolate and pick apart every inch of me.

My own thoughts are tearing me down and
keeping me prisoner here.
Everytime I think I have enough energy I get
reminded that I'm not good enough.
That I am ugly
I am fat.
I am not smart enough to escape.

I retreat back into the cold stillness with only
this blanket and this couch.

I'd do anything to stop the onslaught of thoughts.
Sleep. I must sleep.

A Bright Light

My boy.
I can see his face.
Every now and again.
He will come and visit me.

I feel as if I am in a deep well.
Everytime I look up it seems as if there is a giant
tunnel.
And at the other end of it is my boy.

His face is so animated.
He is talking to me but I can't hear any of the
words coming out of his mouth.
But I can see his face.
I can see the bright light that is shining in his
eyes.
There is so much iife in him for a moment I have
to look away.
Tears block my vision and I have to blink them
away before I can look at him again.

I reach out to try to capture that precious face.
This tunnel, this well, it's so long and I can't
reach him.

I stand on my tiptoes to get a better advantage
and it's no use.
I try to climb up the walls of this well; I claw
and claw until my fingers bleed.

I can see his smile slip abit.
When I can't get out and reach him.
I continue to claw at the sides of my well, my
tunnel.
I will continue to do so until I have no strength.
I hope he comes back again tomorrow.

Anger

My heart.
My head.
Everything is on fire.
The flames are clouding my eyes.

I can't function like this.
I can't do anything.
I have to try and contain this fire.
It's racing through my veins now.

I throw a cooling sheet over me.
I ground myself into the earth.
Into the cooling dirt.
After a while I feel my fire go out.

Flawed

I should be able to handle this.
I should be able to fix this.
I should be able to find a way to get over this.
I should be able to do these things.

The fact that I can't must mean there is
something wrong with me.
The fact that I can't must mean that I am weak.
The fact that I can't must mean that I am a
burden.
The fact that I can't must mean that I don't
deserve anyone's love.

Again

14

Round and round the cycle goes.
It has happened so many times I don't know
what revolution we are on.
I get captured.
I struggle.
I break free.
Then it repeats.
Again and again.
Is there no way to spin me out of this orbit?

Hovel

15

The filth is all around me.
It's in my head.
It's in my heart.
It's beside me.
It opens it's mouth and talks to me.
For a long time that is all I had to listen to.

Burst Wave

My dam keeps cracking.
Everytime I get it built a little higher.
The cracks start at the bottom.
They create a rift all the way to the top.
If I can't keep it repaired my emotions are gunna
collapse the dam.
The burst wave will kill anything and anyone
caught in the path.

Cold

It's cold here.
In my mind.
There is frost on everything.
My motivation is encased in ice.
I have an ice pick.
But the ice is too thick.
And my hands are red and hurting.

Ghost

I'm yelling.
I feel as if my voice is going to go out.
I yell and frantically gesture to anyone passing
by.
They don't hear me.
I need help.
No one can hear me.
I'm all alone.
I'm a ghost.

Okay

It will be okay, sweetheart.
It will be fine, I'm here.
You don't have to worry anymore.
All those times you couldn't get up, forgive
yourself.
All those times you couldn't face your family,
forgive yourself.
All those times you couldn't take a shower,
forgive yourself.
Forgive yourself, because you are back and you
are fighting for yourself again.

Best

Do your best.
That is all you can do.
Save some energy to take care of you.
Replenish your spirit.
If you didn't accomplish your goals, try again.
Don't give up. Stay in the game.
Lose the battle to win the war.

Hope

21

Take a deep breath.
Breathe in that hope.
Let it fill your lungs and feed your heart.
Hold that breath and feel it overtake you.
Then breathe it out and take another.
Each one will heal your soul.

Remember

I remember that that time.
The time that I wanted to live again.
I decided that I was done struggling.
I was done with fighting.
I was done with feeling angry.
I was done with feeling sad.
I wanted to laugh.
The turning of the tide was when I wanted to
laugh.

Strangle

Fights that use to take me days, I can do in
hours.
I can fight to the death with my depression.
I can strangle it everytime now.
Sometimes I can do it immediately.
Sometimes it takes me longer.
But I can do it, and I can live with myself after.

Weight

24

My shoulders do not sag as heavily as they once did.
I can straighten my back and adjust my posture.
I can finally bear the weight and be comfortable.

Laugh

I can stare at the sky and not cry.
The thoughts running through my head don't
make me sad.
I can belly laugh now.
I can laugh so hard my sides hurt and my voice
goes hoarse.
I can help people.
That makes me feel good.
I can participate in life.
I want to participate in life.